Girlfriends

A POSTCARD BOOK™

TWENTY-EIGHT **ZANY** POSTCARDS TO
MAIL TO FRIENDS AND ENEMIES ALIKE!

RUNNING PRESS
PHILADELPHIA · LONDON

Printed in Canada

This book may not be reproduced in whole or in part, in any form or by any means, electronic or mechanical, including photocopying, recording, or by any information storage and retrieval system now known or hereafter invented, without written permission from the publisher.

Postcard Book is a trademark of Running Press Book Publishers.

9   8   7   6   5   4   3   2
Digit on the right indicates the number of this printing

ISBN 0-7624-0087-0

Created by Paul Kepple and Tara Ann McFadden
Picture research by Susan Oyama
Front and back cover photographs: © H. Armstrong Roberts
Title page photograph: © H. Armstrong Roberts

This book may be ordered by mail from the publisher. Please add $2.50 for postage and handling. *But try your bookstore first!*

Running Press Book Publishers
125 South Twenty-second Street
Philadelphia, Pennsylvania 19103-4399

Do you have **SPINACH IN YOUR TEETH?** Put on an **extra five pounds** lately? *Nasty rumors* about your *sex life* running the rumor circuit?

Your girlfriends are always there to comfort you when these mishaps occur—they're also the first to point them out, of course. (Thanks a lot, girls. If I'd wanted **false sympathy,** I'd have **asked a man!)**

Some girlfriends you **TRUST** with your life. Others . . . well, you wouldn't turn your back on them for a minute. But ever since those school days when they told **your secrets** to the boys or wouldn't let you jump rope, you've

 forgiven them. After all, you were all playing by the same rules.

They've been like sisters to you—you've *loved them* and **HATED THEM** from the beginning, and you wouldn't trade them for the world. (If you did you'd be in trouble—they **know everything** you've done and they **can't wait** for an excuse to tell!)

At your best or at your worst, the girls are always there to pick you up or squash you down. Now you can celebrate that bond with this collection of **SHAMELESSLY SPITEFUL** scenes to send to your super-special friends.

I **SWORE** to Betty I wouldn't tell a soul but . . .

Girlfriends

A POSTCARD BOOK™

Girlfriends

A POSTCARD BOOK™

MARLENE
FACE PEEL

DOROTHY
FULL FACIAL
RECONSTRUCTION

ETHEL
COLLAGEN LIPS,
NOSE JOB

ROSALIE
HAIR PLUGS

CANDY
SKIN GRAFT,
GLASS EYE

MYRTLE
MUD MASK, TEETH CAPS

GERTIE
DOUBLE CHIN REMOVED

With a little surgery **YOU** can be a **BEAUTY** too!

Girlfriends

A POSTCARD BOOK™

WHICH HAS MORE PLASTIC:
Marge or her shower curtain?

Girlfriends

A POSTCARD BOOK™

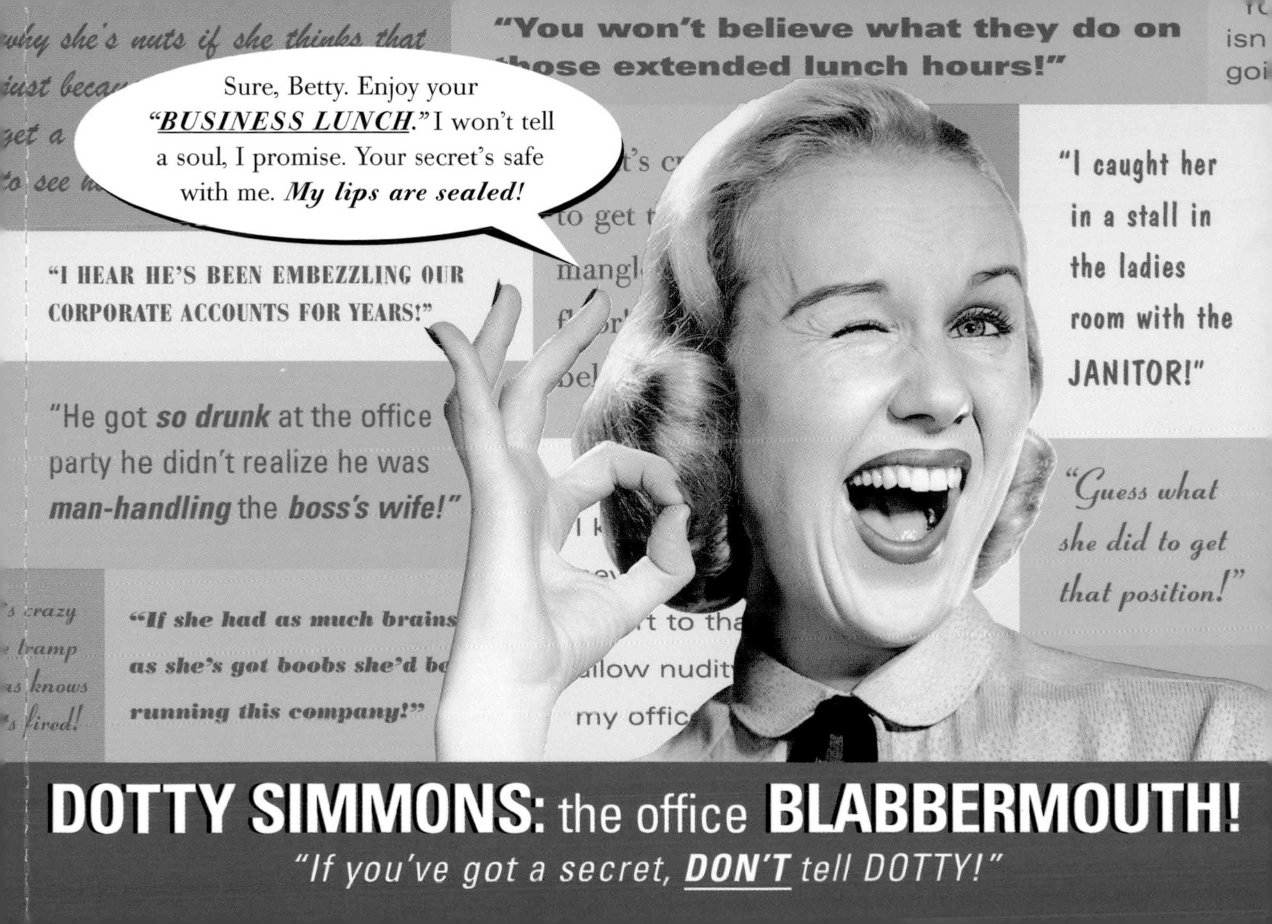
"You won't believe what they do on
those extended lunch hours!"
Sure, Betty. Enjoy your "BUSINESS LUNCH." I won't tell a soul, I promise. Your secret's safe with me. My lips are sealed!
"I HEAR HE'S BEEN EMBEZZLING OUR CORPORATE ACCOUNTS FOR YEARS!"
"I caught her in a stall in the ladies room with the JANITOR!"
"He got so drunk at the office party he didn't realize he was man-handling the boss's wife!"
"Guess what she did to get that position!"
"If she had as much brains as she's got boobs she'd be running this company!"
DOTTY SIMMONS: the office BLABBERMOUTH!
"If you've got a secret, DON'T tell DOTTY!"

Girlfriends

A POSTCARD BOOK™

Girlfriends

A POSTCARD BOOK™

Maybe if I leave the *iron* on, the house will *burn down*, we can collect the *insurance money*, and then I can get a *BETTER* mink stole than that Mabel Jones!

KEEPING UP *with the* JONESES

Girlfriends

A POSTCARD BOOK™

Girlfriends

A POSTCARD BOOK™

Girlfriends

A POSTCARD BOOK™

LOOK AT BARBARA! SHE'S THE PERFECT WOMAN!

HOW DO **YOU** MEASURE UP?

How does she do it?

EYES
BIG BABY BLUES ARE ALWAYS AN ATTENTION GETTER!

TEETH
PEARLY WHITE TO MAKE THAT SMILE SPARKLE!

BOSOMS
PERKY, FIRM, NOT TOO BIG, NOT TOO SMALL.

TUMMY
A TIGHT TUMMY IS A HAPPY TUMMY. SUCK IT IN!

SKIRT
SNUG, FORM FITTING FABRICS GET YOU THOSE SECOND LOOKS!

LEGS
LONG-N-LANKY, WAXED, AND BUFFED TO A PERFECT SHINE!

HAIR
FROSTED, CURLED, AND SPRAYED TO PERFECTION!

WAIST
CINCHED TIGHT FOR MAXIMUM EFFECT!

HIPS
ROUND AND VOLUPTUOUS— A REAL HANDFUL!

APRON
SHOWS YOU'RE DOMESTIC, NOT AFRAID TO COOK-N-CLEAN

KNEES
IF THEY'RE KNOBBY, KEEP 'EM COVERED!

SHOES
HIGH HEELS ONLY! COMFORT DOESN'T REALLY MATTER!

Girlfriends

A POSTCARD BOOK™

Girlfriends

A POSTCARD BOOK™

Girlfriends

A POSTCARD BOOK™

Girlfriends

A POSTCARD BOOK™

AN AVON AFFAIR

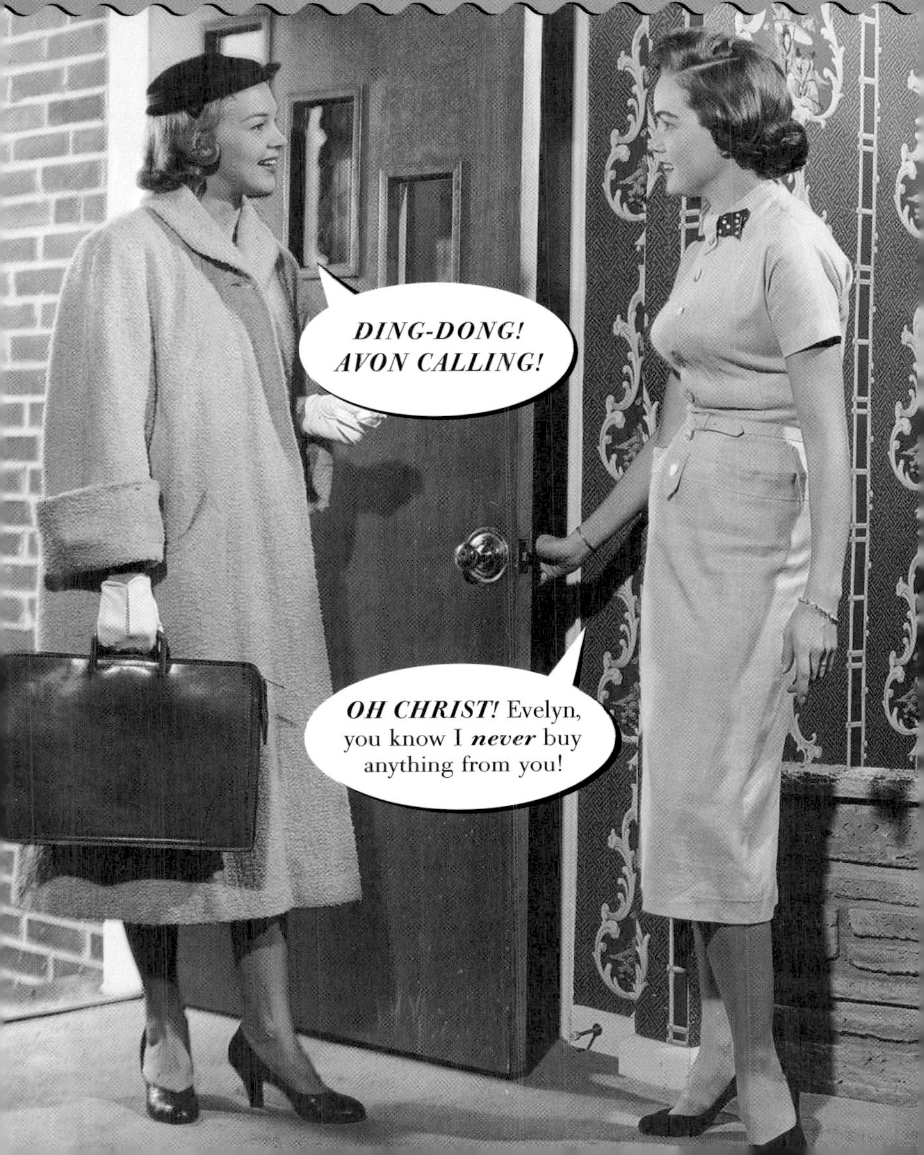

Girlfriends

A POSTCARD BOOK™

Girlfriends

A POSTCARD BOOK™

Mary, would you BELIEVE it got THIS BIG?

Now, just WHAT size are we talking about, Joan?

GIRRRRRRLS?

What's the MATTER, Helen? Can't a girl BRAG about her SOUFFLE?

Girlfriends

A POSTCARD BOOK™

KEEP AWAY from Sally! She **BITES!**
"She's MEAN, she's VICIOUS, and she's <u>PRE-MENSTRUAL!</u>"

Girlfriends

A POSTCARD BOOK™

Girlfriends

A POSTCARD BOOK™

"Here you go, Betty Ramsey's **HEAD**, just like you ordered. That'll **TEACH HER** for using <u>**IMITATION**</u> chocolate in the bake-off."

Girlfriends

A POSTCARD BOOK™

Girlfriends

A POSTCARD BOOK™

Girlfriends

A POSTCARD BOOK™

If Phyllis asks me if I'm a "bottle blond" ***ONE MORE TIME,*** she's gonna get a

KNUCKLE SANDWICH!

Girlfriends

A POSTCARD BOOK™

Girlfriends

A POSTCARD BOOK™

Girlfriends

A POSTCARD BOOK™

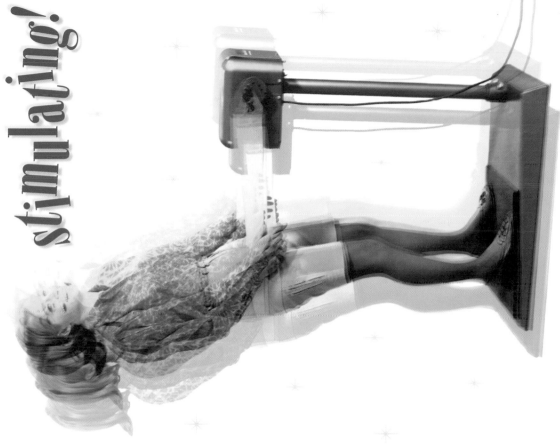

Who EVER thought _EXERCISE_ could be this **stimulating!**

Girlfriends

A POSTCARD BOOK™

Girlfriends

A POSTCARD BOOK™

PARTNERS *in* CRIME

"**I TOLD** you I'd do it Sally. That cheating, no-good finally **DROVE** me to it. Now, help me **GET RID** of the evidence. Want yours **WELL DONE** or **RARE**?"

Girlfriends

A POSTCARD BOOK™

Girlfriends

A POSTCARD BOOK™